Focus on Fine Arts:

ELEMENTARY

Miriam Kronish
Jeryl Abelmann

Frederick B. Tuttle, Jr.
Series Editor

nea PROFESSIONAL LIBRARY
National Education Association
Washington, D.C.

Acknowledgment

The authors wish to thank the following educators for their assistance in developing this publication: Jack Borden, Lexington, Massachusetts; Dr. Rose Feinberg, Needham Public Schools; Judith Grace, Needham, Massachusetts; Delores Larque and Elaine Messias, Needham Public Schools; and Larry White and Dan DeWolf, Needham Science Center.

Printing History
First Printing: September 1989

Note

The opinions expressed in this publication should not be construed as representing the policy or position of the National Education Association. Materials published by the NEA Professional Library are intended to be discussion documents for educators who are concerned with specialized interests of the profession.

Library of Congress Cataloging-in-Publication Data

Kronish, Miriam.
    Elementary / Miriam Kronish, Jeryl Abelmann.
        p.   cm. — (Focus on fine arts)
    Bibliography: p.
    ISBN 0-8106-0301-2
    1. Arts—Study and teaching (Elementary)—United States.
    2. Learning, Psychology of.   I. Abelmann, Jeryl.   II. Title
    III. Series.
    NX305.K76   1989
    372.5043'—dc20   89-9344
                                                            CIP

CONTENTS

Editor's Preface 5

Chapter 1. Overview 13

  The Arts 13
  Integration of the Arts 16

Chapter 2. An Instructional Framework 18

  An Integrated Approach 18
    Case Study 19
  Balance in Teacher Planning 24
  The Role of the Principal 26

Chapter 3. Examining the Curriculum:
Instuctional Format 29

  The 4Mat System 29
  Illustrative Units 35
    Butterflies 35
    Sun Time 37

Chapter 4. Classroom Applications 39

  Three Units 39
    The Battle of the Blue and the Gray 39
    Pirates in the Kindergarten 42
    Casey at the Bat 44

Chapter 5. For Spacious Skies (An Extended Study) 46

  Getting Started 46
  Integrated Activities for Music 50
  Integrated Activities for Visual Arts 51
  Student and Staff Products 53
  Conclusion 55

Bibliography 56

The Authors

Miriam Kronish is Principal, John Eliot School, Needham, Massachusetts.

Jeryl Abelmann is a fifth grade teacher in the San Ramon Valley Unified School District, Danville, California.

The Series Editor

Frederick B. Tuttle, Jr., is Assistant Superintendent, Needham Public Schools, Massachusetts. A former university professor and education consultant, Dr. Tuttle is the author of *Composition: A Media Approach, Gifted and Talented Students*, and *How to Prepare Students for Writing Tests*; the editor of *Fine Arts in the Curriculum*; and the coauthor of *Technical and Scientific Writing, Characteristics and Identification of Gifted and Talented Students*, and *Program Design and Development for Gifted and Talented Students*, all published by NEA. He also developed the NEA multimedia program *Educating Gifted and Talented Students*.

The Advisory Panel

Wayne R. Bauman, Elementary Counselor, Douglas Elementary School, Des Moines, Iowa

Michael E. Crane, Head Teacher, Pomona School, Galloway Township, New Jersey

Kathy A. Norris, Kindergarten Teacher, Peter Crump Elementary School, Montgomery, Alabama

Barry W. Thomas, Classroom Teacher, Pleasant Plains Elementary School, Towson, Maryland

Marian Trainor, Media Specialist, Wilkerson School, Warren Consolidated Schools, Michigan

EDITOR'S PREFACE

American people are today concerned with humanistic and cultural matters to a degree unprecedented in their history. [Far] from reflecting this new concern with humanistic and cultural matters, the schools of the nation have let the humanities and the arts languish. (10)*

THE ARTS ARE BASIC

The position of the performing and visual arts in our educational system has not improved appreciably since Alvin Eurich made this observation in 1969. While few would deny the value of the arts, many continually relegate them to the periphery of curricula in most schools. In 1985 the national Parent Teachers Association found that—

Nearly 70 percent of the 1,164 schools recently surveyed by the Alliance of Independent Colleges of Art have experienced cuts in art teachers, courses or program budgets since 1981. Forty percent of these schools expect even further cuts.

Only about 2 percent of the average school budget is spent on arts programs. . . .

Knowledge and skills in music have decreased by 3.3 percent among 9-year-olds and 2.5 percent among 17-year-olds in the past seven years. (10)

To effect a substantive change we need not only a reaffirmation of the importance of the arts, but also practical descriptions of ways that they can begin to fulfill their roles in the educational process. The National Endowment for the Arts gives direction to this need:

Basic arts education must give students the essence of our civilization, the civilizations which have contributed to ours, and the more distant civilizations which enrich world civilizations as a whole. It must also give students tools for creating, for communicating and understanding others' communications, and for making informal and critical choices. (9, p. 13)

Importance of the Arts

Education in the arts plays a major role in three general areas of

---

*Numbers in parentheses appearing in this Preface refer to the References on page 11.

educational impact: societal, instructional, and individual. "[One] of the major goals of education should be to promote the continuation of culture, transmitting values and concepts of civilization from one generation to the next" (13). Through study of the arts we may acquire a cultural record of our past and present. This understanding is necessary to help put ourselves and our value systems into perspective. The necessity of such a perspective has been acknowledged by William Bennett, former secretary of education:

> All students, then, should know some of these works [of art] for a simple reason: they cannot understand the present if they have no understanding of the past. If we cut them off from our culture's past, we automatically make youth aliens in their own culture. And that makes them ill-equipped to succeed in or even understand the world around them. (3)

While students gain knowledge of events and historical movements that shaped society, they also gain insights into the underlying value systems and beliefs of societies and cultures through the arts. "[Humans] experience and give expression to their most deeply held values, beliefs, and images through the arts, and there can be no adequate form of general education that does not include them" (12).

Instructionally, the arts may provide both creative outlets for students to express themselves as well as alternative avenues through which students may understand others' feelings and ideas. Some teachers base their interpretations of a student's learnings primarily on performance on "objective" tests, written essays, or class participation. However, many students who do not perform well through these means are able to show that they understand a concept when encouraged to respond through other means such as art, photography, drama, and dance (14). Ultimately, students must learn how to communicate effectively through tests and essays if they are to succeed in our educational system. But some students must first acquire confidence in themselves. Once they are able to demonstrate that they do understand the concepts, these students often transfer this confidence to responses through other, more "academic," means. Indeed, once a student shows understanding of a concept, the instructional task changes. Instead of stressing the concept itself, the teacher may then focus on the mode of expression.

Moreover, some students learn particular concepts more effectively through the arts than through textbooks and lectures. While developing a program using films and pictures to teach poetry, for example, I found that many students for whom the poems were considered too difficult could accurately state the themes of the poems when they were presented visually in films. I concluded that "once the students have found they can read visual images accompanying a poem, they can [often] read and react critically to the poem itself [in its printed version]" (15). Robert Spillane, Superintendent of Fairfax County (Virginia) Public Schools, summarizes the importance of the arts to all education:

> In any case, an education and a life that ignore vast areas of expression, communication, conceptualization, and innovation—the visual and aural areas—will surely hamstring our future communicators, conceptualizers, and innovators. . . . Thus, education must give space—albeit in a crowded curriculum—to the arts, which connect thinking and feeling in the aural and visual worlds. (12).

The inability of students and teachers to draw connections among disciplines has resulted in a fragmentation of learning. As students progress from one grade level to the next, this isolation of studies increases. Ernest Boyer, President of the Carnegie Foundation for the Advancement of Teaching, comments on the role arts education may play in overcoming this departmentalization of learning:

> After visiting colleges and schools, I am convinced that students at all levels need to see connections. And I believe that finding patterns across separate disciplines can be accomplished through the arts. . . . I'm suggesting that the arts give us a language that cuts across the disciplines, help us to see connections and bring a more coherent meaning to our world. (4)

Perhaps the greatest benefit of arts education is to the student as an individual. The "arts can provide the means for communicating thoughts, emotions, and ideas that cannot otherwise be expressed. The arts also contribute significantly to each individual's search for identity, self-realization, and personal confidence" (12). One of the outcomes of the "visual literacy" movement in the 1970s was the introduction of filmmaking as part of many curricula. Students who had previously considered dropping out of school began to use film to share their ideas and feelings with teachers and classmates. They became recognized and valued in the academic envi-

7

ronment because they could interact effectively with others. For the first time they encountered success instead of failure in school. Boyer places this role of the arts at the top of his list: "First, the arts are needed in the nation's schools because they help children express feelings and ideas words cannot convey" (4).

For those students who have particular aptitude in the arts, the inclusion of the arts in education is especially vital. As Elliot Eisner, Professor of Art and Education at Stanford University, observes,

> The inclusion of the arts in the school's curriculum provides opportunity not only for all students to learn to read the arts, but especially for those students whose aptitudes are in the arts. . . . It is hard to discover what one doesn't have an opportunity to practice. Educational equity is an empty ideal when a substantial portion of our children are excluded from the very areas in which their talents reside. (6)

Although the importance of the arts in education has been generally acknowledged for these and other reasons, in most schools the arts are still treated as "frill" areas of the curriculum with the basic instruction focusing on language, mathematics, science, and social studies. When a budget crisis strikes, as it did in California with Proposition 13 and in Massachusetts with Proposition 2 1/2, arts education usually suffers through severe budget cuts or even elimination. Eisner offers several reasons for the marginal position of arts in the curriculum. Among these are views that (1) the arts are emotional, not cognitive; (2) lack of assessment in the arts; (3) the arts are solely creative experiences; and (4) the arts are innate rather then learned (6). To place education in the arts closer to the center of the curriculum, we must address these views and realistically demonstrate vital roles the arts may play within academic curricula. As Bennett states, "Those of us engaged in education must promote the truth that study of the arts increases both our individual capacities for creativity and love for the highest creative work of others" (2).

Underlying Assumptions for the Fine Arts Series

The basic premise for developing this series of monographs on the arts in the classroom is that to accomplish the preservation and transmission of knowledge, skill, values, and culture from generation to generation, we must address the study of the humanities, including the study of visual and performing arts. Four assumptions underlie this premise:

1. All students should have both exposure to and instruction in visual and performing arts throughout elementary and secondary education.
2. Curricula in the visual and performing arts should be presented both as unique disciplines in themselves as well as integral components of other disciplines where appropriate.
3. As with any discipline, visual and performing arts curricula should follow a sequential, organized pattern from kindergarten through grade 12.
4. Finally, the effectiveness of programs and student achievement in visual and performing arts should be assessed based on the program and content of the curricula.

Instruction should not be limited only to those students who display particular talents in the arts. As the National PTA states: "Art is basic to life. It helps us understand ourselves and others. It provides comfort and pleasure through books, music, film, painting and the performing and decorative arts" (10). All students should have the opportunity to enjoy and learn from the arts. Exposure alone is not sufficient, however. "Appreciating a work of art demands intelligent application of perceptual and cognitive resources" (11). Such learning calls for direct instruction.

This instruction should be developmental and sequential from elementary through secondary school, with each year building upon learnings of a previous year. Describing the Discipline-Based Art Education program, Eisner states:

> If a sound art education program were implemented effectively in schools from kindergarten through twelfth grade, youngsters finishing school would be more artistically literate.... Youngsters finishing schooling would understand something about the relationships between culture and the content and form of art. (5)

Too often many educators treat art education as either a separate study isolated from other disciplines or only in relation to other disciplines. Both approaches are necessary for students to learn the content of visual and performing arts as well as the integral relationships between the arts and other disciplines. While the visual and performing arts are disciplines in themselves with their own

9

contents, they are also integral to many other disciplines. When studied in support of other disciplines, however, the arts tend to be viewed only as illustrations of concepts in the more "academic" studies, with little attention being paid to their own content. Consequently, education in the arts should be approached in both ways: as separate disciplines and in relation to other disciplines.

Unless the effectiveness of arts programs is legitimately assessed, work in those curricula will not be highly valued. As Eisner observes, "What we test is what we teach" (6). Consequently, program evaluation should assess the validity of the content, the effectiveness of instruction and, especially, student achievement. Since most student achievement in the visual and performing arts does not lend itself to traditional evaluation procedures, many arts educators base their evaluation on effort rather than actual achievement. As with other disciplines, however, students should be held to appropriate standards and expectations related directly to the instruction and content. In Project Zero, for example, which emphasizes student production, the assessment procedures focus on projects, portfolios, and interviews concentrating on the students' creative processes (8, 15). In the Discipline-Based Arts Education program, "Evaluation of outcomes pertains not only to the products of the students' efforts—the skills, the newfound appreciations, the fresh understandings, the refined judgment that students achieve—but also to the way in which students are engaged in the process of learning" (6). Each program should design its own assessment procedure based on the content of the discipline and the goals of the instructional approach. In the report *Toward Civilization*, the National Endowment for the Arts stresses the importance of assessment in the arts: "Without testing and evaluation, there is no way to measure individual and program progress, program objectives will lack specificity, the arts courses will continue to be considered extracurricular and unimportant" (9, p. 27).

—Frederick B. Tuttle, Jr.
Series Editor

REFERENCES

1. "Arts Education: A Position Statement and Proposed Action." Boston: Board of Education, Commonwealth of Massachusetts, 1975.

2. Bennett, William J. "The Flap." Speech given at National Association of Schools of Music National Convention, Colorado Springs, Colorado, November 24, 1986.

3. _____."Why the Arts Are Essential." *Educational Leadership* 45, no. 4, January 1988.

4. Boyer, Ernest L. *"The Arts, Language and the Schools."* *Basic Education* 2, no. 4, Summer 1987.

5. Eisner, Elliot. "On Discipline-Based Art Education: A Conversation with Elliot Eisner." *Educational Leadership* 45, no. 4, January 1988.

6. _____. *The Role of Discipline-Based Art Education in America's Schools.* Los Angeles: Getty Center for Education in the Arts, 1986.

7. _____. "Why Arts Are Basic." *Basic Education* 31, no. 9, May 1987.

8. Gardner, Howard. "On Assessment in the Arts: A Conversation with Howard Gardner." *Educational Leadership* 45, no. 4, January 1988.

9. National Endowment for the Arts. *Toward Civilization: A Report on Arts Education.* Washington, D.C.: U.S. Government Printing Office, May 1988.

10. National Parent Teachers Association. *Children and the Arts: What Your PTA Can Do.* Chicago: the Association, 1985.

11. Perkins, D. N. "Art as an Occasion of Intelligence." *Educational Leadership* 45, no. 4, January 1988.

12. Spillane, Robert R. "Arts Education Is Not a Frill." Updating School Board Policies. Alexandria, Va.: National School Boards Association, 1987.

13. Tuttle, Frederick B., Jr. ed. *Fine Arts in the Curriculum.* Washington, D.C.: National Education Association, 1985.

14. _____. "Robert's Problem . . . or Ours?—Visuals in the Classroom." *Connecticut English Journal,* Fall 1978.

15. _____. "Visualizing Poetry." *Media and Methods,* May 1970.

16. Wise, Joseph. "Music as a Catalyst for Inter-Disciplinary Education: Attitudes of School Administrators." *ERS Spectrum* 5, no. 2, Spring 1987.

17. Wolf, Dennie Palmer. "Opening Up Assessment." *Educational Leadership* 45, no. 4, January 1988

NEA POLICY
ON FINE ARTS EDUCATION

Resolution C-24. Fine Arts Education

The National Education Association believes that artistic expression is basic to an individual's intellectual, aesthetic, and emotional development. The Association therefore believes that every elementary and secondary school curriculum must include a balanced comprehensive, and sequential program of fine arts instruction taught by educators certified in those fields.

The Association urges its state affiliates to become involved in the promotion, expansion, and implementation of a fine arts program in the curriculum. (80, 87)

Chapter 1

OVERVIEW

THE ARTS

The arts are basic—within our schools and within our lives. As we integrate the arts from the preschool level through graduate school, we find that we are enabling students to develop their creativity and their ability to reason, to draw abstractions, to analyze, to give personal meaning to what they are learning, and to express themselves in very powerful and fulfilling ways. An educated person is one who is able to think—both creatively and critically. One of the best ways to foster this process is through the arts.

It is also critical that we establish a balanced curriculum—one in which the arts and the sciences are equally represented. As Arthur Efland points out,

> When the arts are found to be strong, it is likely that the total program has quality, as well. Conversely, if strength in the arts is lacking, other parts of the program are equally wanting, for the quality of the arts is a barometer that serves to indicate the levels of economic support for the total school program. (1)*

Students show us where they are developmentally as they produce their drawings, their paintings, their stories, their dramatic improvisations, their dances, their poetry. As we study their products, we understand how they make sense of their world. Through the arts, we help them incorporate what we are teaching into their lives. We enable them to express themselves in a variety of ways—verbally, nonverbally, musically, artistically, scientifically, mathematically. We encourage learners to experiment, to take risks, to venture into the unknown, to make mistakes and profit from them, to employ different modalities to demonstrate their newly acquired knowledge.

---

*Numbers in parentheses appearing in the text refer to the Bibliography on page 56.

Throughout the 1980s, the studies of learning styles delineated various approaches to learning that students employ. Some learners are most comfortable when they are actively at work "doing." Others are more comfortable in a reflective mode—listening to the teacher. Some would rather take what they have learned to a higher level, while still others must talk it through before it can have any relevance to them. This understanding that students must be taught with a variety of approaches has a direct application to curriculum development. Experiential learning—testing theories, creating models, tinkering, expressing ideas visually, aurally, and kinesthetically—reinforces the learner as well as the concepts. When students show how much they have understood via a poem or a piece of prose, a picture or a painting, their self-concept is strengthened; a sense of self-worth and dignity is fostered. To be understood fully by all students, an idea or concept must be presented in a variety of ways—orally, in writing, musically, visually— the more dimensions that are utilized, the more deeply ingrained the idea or concept will become.

Kindergartners, for example, learn about animals by listening to stories about them, drawing pictures, singing songs, moving like animals, taking field trips to a local farm or zoo, writing their own stories and big books about animals, listening to guest speakers and asking them questions about animals, having animals visit their classrooms, looking at films, listening to tapes, sculpting animals, and translating concepts into dramatic play. Young students approach reality through their imagination. The arts are an integral part of how they learn. Through the arts they learn at the outset that their ideas are important, that their ideas have value. As they share their products with their peers, they learn from each other.

Just as it is important for students to share their ideas and products with each other, so it is important for teachers and specialists, curriculum directors and principals to come together to plan the total curriculum from kindergarten throughout the elementary grades. As the teacher and the art specialist interact, each can learn from the other how to broaden and deepen the subject. As the music teacher and the classroom teacher engage in long-range planning, the music that students will be learning will incorporate the content of the disciplines (i.e., social studies and language arts). As the media specialist and the principal sit down together to enrich the school's program, the major themes at each grade level will be actualized by adding books to the school library that will complement the classroom materials. As the curriculum directors meet with each other, the opportunities for making connections from one discipline to another—an interdisciplinary approach—can become a reality. Teaching is often a lonely profession. Unless one is team-teaching, the teacher is usually working alone in a self-contained classroom.

When a school begins to integrate the curriculum, professionals begin to communicate collaboratively, constructing bridges from one level to the next, from one discipline to another. People learn from each other. Curriculum is strengthened and students are the beneficiaries. We see this in terms of quality of product, as well as in terms of test scores. We see students who had great difficulty in reading learning to read through poetry. We see students who had a poor self-image stand tall as they demonstrate their musical ability in the school band. We see the teacher who has artistic talent sharing it with colleagues, enhancing the aesthetic environment of the school, using this talent to embellish worksheets and turn them into "worth" sheets.

Toward Civilization: A Report on Arts Education cites four major reasons for art education:

- To understand civilization
- To develop creativity
- To learn the tools of communication
- To develop the capacity for making wise choices among the products of the arts. (7)

According to Elliot Eisner, a first virtue of an effective arts education is helping students learn to see what they look at, hear what they listen to, and feel what they touch.

A second virtue of effective arts education is to help students stretch their minds beyond the literal and the rule-governed....When well taught, the arts free the mind from rigid certainty....What could be more critical to any society seeking multiple solutions to the myriad problems before it? (2, p. 10)

Literacy in the arts means that students need to learn to read and interpret the varied meanings of poetry, music, visual arts, and

15

dance. Through the arts, they find meaningful access to their cultural heritage. The arts require a sensing mind in order to live. They are part of the articulated goal commitment of most states. They have played a key role in human history, as well as in our daily lives.

Thus, the artistic and expressive are part of the normal developmental processes of human beings. John Goodlad and Jack Morrison outline the role of the schools in relation to arts education as follows:

> The arts offer access to virtually infinite environmental complexity. Insightful modern educators suggest incorporating the arts in general education to... among many other reasons, challenge that part of the brain not actively engaged by many other kinds of stimuli....The arts widely used in the schools offer a means of creating and sharing commonly held experiences. The arts are basic, intrinsic, an integral part of the curriculum and of our lives. (3, p. 18)

INTEGRATION OF THE ARTS

As we think about our own educational background, what do we remember as outstanding? A special field trip? A school concert or play? A piece of sculpture on display? A debut as a musician? The first poem we wrote when we never thought we could? A painting hung so proudly on the refrigerator for all to admire? Dancing with classmates on the school playground with hundreds of onlookers applauding wildly? Playing the cymbals in the kindergarten band?

The arts create a deeper dimension; they flood the senses, engrave their images, enliven the spirit, challenge the intellect, enrich the curriculum as they enable the learner to make greater sense out of what is presented in the classroom.

As teachers, we seek to understand, clarify, make the complex simple, the unknown known. We forge a partnership with students as we learn with them and from them. We strive to enable the learner to form a link to the subject, creating a balance between the logical and sequential on one side and the holistic and simultaneous on the other. The arts play a key role as an intrinsic component of the curriculum from preschool through graduate school and throughout life. As students learn, it is natural for them to experiment, to improvise, to adapt, and to augment what they are learning. As they work to understand concepts and ideas, they manipulate and personalize them. They play with them; they relate them to other ideas; they alter them. In short, they take ideas and make them their own. They show that they understand by expressing themselves in a variety of ways, often other than the ways they were taught. The arts can provide an important vehicle for this task. Writing songs to illustrate mathematical ideas, painting pictures of the ocean as the Pilgrims might have seen it during their perilous crossing, improvising a skit to depict the writing of the United States Constitution are but a few illustrations. The more the teacher integrates activities, the more the student can become actively involved in a personal way. Drawing connections from one subject to another, linked by the arts as an intrinsic component, forges a powerful bond that reinforces the concepts, expands the horizons, and ensures that the learner will have a deeper understanding and find personal meaning in what is being taught.

Integrated education involves connection making. Through integration, we look at the curriculum as a unified whole—a gestalt—rather than as a series of isolated subject areas. Subjects do not exist in a vacuum. They are linked from one discipline to another. Mathematics merges with music, social studies with singing, language arts with lettering, science with sculpting. The power of the arts as an integrating catalyst is dramatic and compelling. The arts help students to produce individual works, reach for self-discovery, and acquire self-satisfaction, products that reinforce the learner's sense of self-worth and dignity.

Too often we view subjects as a list of content areas to be "covered" one after another. With the integrated approach, whenever appropriate, we view each subject as part of a greater whole, each contributing to and building upon other subjects.

Chapter 2

AN INSTRUCTIONAL FRAMEWORK

AN INTEGRATED APPROACH

Schematically, the subjects in an integrated approach are viewed as shown in Figure 1. As each area is included within the major theme ("topic"), the learner's understanding is deepened. The drawing of connections brings clarity, and opportunities for creative work. A painting can lead to scientific inquiry. A poem can serve as a springboard to a social studies discussion. A song, composed by students, can demonstrate mathematical principles. No subject stands in isolation. Each area becomes linked. Within every discipline lie seeds that can germinate into full-blown blossoms; a cross-pollenization of areas creates a fertile ground that is rewarding to both teacher and student.

The interdisciplinary approach has many strengths. It enables learners to take an active part in their own learning. It challenges

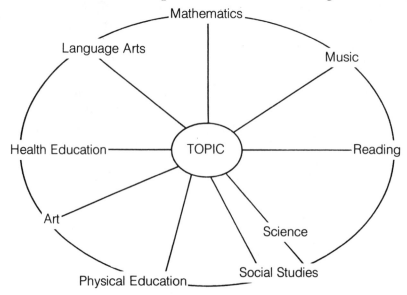

Figure 1
Curriculum Web

18

the creativity of the teacher, as well as that of the students. It stimulates individual inquiry, critical thinking, artistic expression. It helps students make more sense out of a world that at times can be very confusing. One area brings clarity to another. It is motivating. It generates energy. It provides direction and structure. It activates the student's inner resources. Teachers who use this approach find that it generates enthusiasm and excitement for teaching and learning.

The following case study illustrates how a topic—Balance—can provide the vehicle for an integrated lesson.

Case Study

Balance: An Integrated Lesson
(contributed by Karin Alexander, Teacher,
John Baldwin Elementary School, Danville, California)

Background for Students: Balance, symmetry, design, and proportion are qualities that are all around us, yet we often take them for granted. For example, our own bodies are examples of balance, symmetry, and proportion. Our right side is just like our left; the distance from our shoulders to our elbows is about the same as from our elbows to our wrists, upper leg to knees, and knees to ankles. We enjoy and feel comfortable with balance; few people, for example, would enjoy wearing a different shoe on each foot.

In nature all the details of people, animals, and plants are compiled to form one interesting object or being. Everything around us, natural or made by humans, is a compilation of many lines and colors. Our eyes organize these lines and color designs and give shape to the whole object. One might think that this bombardment of lines and colors can be confusing, but instead it is stimulating. The variety of detail, patterns, and designs that our world has to offer stimulates our minds and our senses.

Besides symmetry and balance in nature, we also see it in our human-made environment. Houses and buildings, for example, show symmetry, design, balance, and proportion. Besides an aesthetic standpoint, without such balance our buildings would not withstand the elements of weather or the traffic of people. Careful planning goes into the design of the initial foundation, selection of materials, placement of windows, doors, etc. In the absence of such planning, a building or home may not be functional or long-lasting, much less attractive to a prospective buyer.

Cars are another example of balance, design, symmetry, and proportion. Without the balance of one side with the other, the vehicle would not be functional. The creative designs of each year's new models add aesthetic beauty and charm as well. The following activities recognize balance and symmetry around us:

- Hold up a large picture of a person and have students note the balance previously cited (e.g., two eyes, two arms).
- Cut an orange, an apple, a green pepper in half and have students provide examples of balance.
- Have students work in pairs, citing examples of balance and symmetry around the room.
- Ask students to find examples within their neighborhood or within their homes that exemplify concepts of balance, proportion, and symmetry. They could go to the grocery store, supermarket, pharmacy, toy store. After discussing their findings, they could show what they found using photography, crayons, paint, or clay.

Other activities can help students recognize balance and symmetry in the performing and visual arts. We see symmetry and design in nature in all plants and animals. This aesthetic beauty pleases all our senses. In music, it might be called rhythm; in art, we call it balance, symmetry, design, and proportion.

The folksong "De Grey Goose"* illustrates design, balance, and proportion:

Preacher went a-huntin',
Lord, Lord, Lord.
Carried 'long his shotgun,
Lord, Lord, Lord.
'Long came a grey goose,
Lord, Lord, Lord.
Gun went a -boo-loo,
Lord, Lord, Lord.
Down came a grey goose,
Lord, Lord, Lord.
He was six weeks a-fallin',
Lord, Lord, Lord.
Then they gave a feather pickin',
Lord, Lord, Lord.

*Words and Music by Huddie Ledbetter. Collected and adapted by John A. and Alan Lomax. TRO—© Copyright 1959 (renewed 1987) Folkways Music Publishers, Inc., New York, N.Y. Used by permission.

As students sing this song, they form two groups of equal size. The first group sings the line, the second group, the refrain. Then they switch. As they sing, they feel the design, balance, and proportion. Group one sits down after each line; group two sits down after each refrain. The up-and-down motion accentuates the balance.

We turn to the drawing by Karin Alexander (see Figure 2). After students have had an opportunity to study it closely, ask them to work in pairs and list examples of balance and symmetry that they find. Share their ideas with the whole group and write them on the board.

The class could discuss such questions as, What has the artist done to lend balance and design to her drawing? Where does your eye go first? Second? Why? Do your eyes travel equally around the drawing? The drawing could be used as the stimulus for a visual arts activity.

Activities to recognize balance and symmetry in traditional curricula would be a natural outgrowth of such a discussion. In literature, myths, fairytales, folktales abound with concepts of balance. Balance can be found in "Hansel and Gretel" as students contrast the evil of the stepmother and the witch with the goodness of the children and their father. The gingerbread house in this fairytale is an example of symmetry—windows on either side of the door, curtains at the windows, the roof, the walls. Proportion and balance abound in the illustrations. There is a direct ratio in the story from what Hansel eats as he is force-fed in captivity to the amount of additional weight he puts on as he is asked by the witch to stick out his finger. In some versions of the story, the witch had captured other children and transformed them into other creatures or objects. As the spell is broken, each creature/object becomes a living child. Direct proportion—creature to child—1:1. There is a balance between day and night in the story—the walk into the woods during the day when the children knew their way and into the darkness of the woods at night when they lost their way. For each dropped crumb to help them find their way back, there was a bird to eat the crumb. One-to-one correspondence applies here very nicely.

Poetry is word balance. The following poem was written by Briana Foley, age 10, a fifth grader at the Green Valley Elementary School in Danville, California:

21

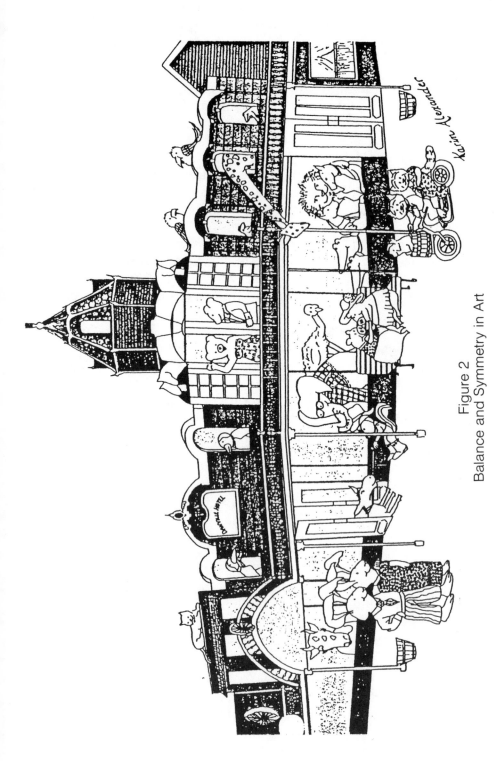

Figure 2
Balance and Symmetry in Art

A Scary Night

Thunder
Long, Noisy
Makes Scary Travels
Sky, Lightning, Thunder, Clouds
Disappears, Shocks, Appears
Scraggly, Yellow
Lightning
BOOM!
Lightning
Big, Small
BOOM!
Flashes, Expands, Appears
Sky, Night, Noise, Sky
Sounds, Gives, Makes
Loud, Short
Thunder
BOOM!

In mathematics, balanced equations, addition and subtraction, ratio, proportion are prime examples of balance. Students in the primary grades learn to add and subtract. Using balance as the focus of the math lesson, the teacher could show "balance" in the following examples:

$$2 + 2 = 4$$

$$4 - 2 = 2$$

The numerals can be represented by people—for example, two students plus two more students equals four students. The class looks at the two groups of two and the four students on the other side of the equation and sees the balance on each side. They will immediately be shown the inverse:

$$4 - 2 = 2$$

Using students again to represent the numerals, four students stand in front of the class. Two leave the group; two remain. Balance is shown as students make the connection between addition and subtraction. One process is the inverse of the other:

$$2 + 2 = 4 \qquad\qquad 4 - 2 = 2$$

In science the butterfly, snowflakes, physical laws depict balance and proportion. To show symmetry in nature, for example, have students go outside on a snowy day, catch a snowflake on a dark piece of paper or cloth and look at it through a magnifying glass. The perfect symmetry is immediately apparent. Studying a butterfly's or moth's markings will also demonstrate symmetry as students observe the colors and shapes and begin to recognize the various species. Hatching a butterfly in the classroom by setting up a cocoon in a butterfly cage can be a very exciting and enlightening experience.

In social studies students learn about the balance of power as our system of government is based on balance among the legislative, judicial, and executive branches. While studying how a bill becomes a law, students learn how the balance of power works. They might become interested in a particular issue to the point where they would like to sponsor a bill. As they follow their bill from first draft to final enactment, they see that there are various forces that directly affect their piece of legislation. They learn that no one branch of government has power over the other; they exist in balance with each other. This is the essence of our democratic form of government.

BALANCE IN TEACHER PLANNING

As the teacher is using these terms—balance, proportion, symmetry—each subject presented during the duration of the unit should be examined for these qualities. Students should be challenged to see where the balance can be found. Balance should also be found within the pages of a teacher's planbook—a balance between the arts and the sciences. A way to check for this is to use a simple outline and to fill in the blanks where appropriate. At the outset of the course of study, how can the arts be integrated into the basic curriculum? In applying integrated planning to their teaching, a group of elementary teachers used the following procedure. First, they brainstormed this list of teaching elements:

Art Activities

Books

Computer Applications

Cooking

Crafts

Dance

Discussions

Dramatic Activities

Evaluation Activities

Field Trips

Games

Guest Speakers

Health and Safety Activities

Homework

Journal Writing

Library/Research

Mathematics

Media/Tapes/Records/Video

Mentors

Movement and Mime Activities

Music

Painting

Peer Teaching

Photography

Physical Education Activities

Poetry

Puzzles

Reading Aloud/Silently

Science

Sculpture

Social Studies

Songs

Spelling

Stories

Vocabulary

Writing

Then, using this list, the teachers made connections from one area to the next, all within the context of the day-to-day program. After considering all the relationships, they made notes beside each area that was appropriate and added new ideas to their repertoire.

Using "red" as the topic for class study, they made the following notes beside each of these areas to be incorporated:

Art—crayons, markers, paints

Books—*The Red Balloon, The Little Red Hen*

Computer Applications—writing their own red stories and publishing them

Cooking—borscht, candied apples

Crafts—woodworking, painting it red

Dance—using "The Red Shoes" music and dancing

Discussions—about the color red, finding synonyms

Dramatic Activities—acting out the story

Evaluation Activities—students' use of new vocabulary, research skills, using a dictionary and thesaurus

This example illustrates how the outline can provide a guide for ensuring connection making, continuity, and integration. A teacher might not use every area, but would have many links to the main theme as the course of study progresses.

Of equal importance to the teacher's planning is students' understanding of the integrated approach. At the onset of the unit, students should engage in curriculum webbing (see Figure 1, p. 18). With the topic/theme in the center of a large sheet of paper, the teacher should lead the class in a discussion of all the areas that touch upon the theme. The main points should be written down and posted for students to use as a guide. As they become more involved, they will continue to add new avenues of exploration. These will be linked to what is already listed, forming a more complex webbing. This enables students to see the big picture with all its spinoffs and ramifications, as the teacher sees the long-range and short-term plans in the planbook.

It is important to enlist the support of the school community, including parents and, especially, principals. Outreach to the community is vital. Teachers and principals can invite parents in to help make the arts a vital part of the life of the school. The school's philosophy/statement of purpose should be clearly articulated to the entire community. At the outset, parents should be oriented to the balance between the arts and the sciences within the school program. When parents are welcomed as partners, exciting things can happen. Parents can become school volunteers; they can share their talents with their children. They can raise money for arts projects, create an after-school activities program, share their expertise with classes when their particular area of interest is being studied. The variety of possibilities is endless. But, for involvement, leadership is the key. School bulletins should inform the community about what is happening and how to become involved, when appropriate.

THE ROLE OF THE PRINCIPAL

As we look at how schools are organized, how curriculum is designed and implemented, and how students learn, we recognize the crucial role that elementary school principals play. A checklist for elementary principals was developed by the National Art Education Association. Broadening the base to include all the arts, the key areas outlined were—

School Leadership
Financial Support
Arts Curricula
Arts Instruction
Arts Personnel
Professional Development
Time and Scheduling
Classroom Materials and Resources
Supplies and Equipment (7, p. 34)

It is imperative that school principals demonstrate leadership. They can show their commitment to the arts by providing support in a variety of ways. Paying attention to the aesthetic environment of the school and ensuring that displays both within the classroom and throughout the building reflect the artistic talent of all students are important aspects of the principal's support for the arts. When the principal models direct involvement in the arts, financial support is more likely to be forthcoming from a variety of sources. The parent-teacher organization also plays a major role in supporting programs both within the school curriculum and in extracurricular events and activities. The principal's suggestions and advice to the parents' organization at budget deliberation time make a crucial difference; they will influence funding decisions for the school. If the principal says, "Why don't we try to fund an artist-in-residence program?" the parents will plan fundraisers and find the most appropriate artist to invite to their school. When parents know that the arts are important to the instructional leader and the staff, the arts will be important to them as well.

As the educational leader, the principal reviews curriculum materials, guides, and texts, and makes recommendations. In school systems that have a professional development account, teachers are hired during the summer to write curricula and plan new programs for inclusion in the fall. A portion of professional development monies could and should be channeled to the arts. Teachers and specialists writing curriculum guides could provide classroom teachers with ideas and materials to strengthen the current courses of study by adding integrated arts activities. Principals play a key role in budgetary disbursements; they should be advocates for the arts. Field trips to local museums, theaters, and concert halls demonstrate the importance of the arts in the cultural life of students and their teachers. The principal can create the climate within which the arts can grow and flourish as cultural field trips become integral components of the curriculum.

In sum, the principal can make a vital difference. In one elementary school where the principal is an arts advocate, the sense of the depth of involvement is obvious in many ways: the corridors are filled with student work, framed prints are strategically hung, murals depict what the school values. Arts fairs are held annually. After-school activity groups including drama, calligraphy, painting, and origami are offered to students and organized by the parent group. Field trips to the ballet and symphony, as well as to theaters and museums, are an integral part of the school curriculum. The staff and parents jointly sponsor a biannual talent show featuring students and teachers. It was not always so. Involvement in the arts began when the principal made a concerted effort to integrate the arts at every grade level.

When the arts are alive and well, students' abilities flourish. They can express themselves so much more deeply when they have been taught via an integrated arts approach. Their sensitivity and understanding are paramount. And the beauty of this approach is that it will form a foundation that will remain with students throughout their lives.

Chapter 3

EXAMINING THE CURRICULUM: INSTRUCTIONAL FORMAT

THE 4MAT SYSTEM

This chapter addresses the learning styles of both teachers and students. Using a particular model of instruction—the 4Mat System—it examines the way students are taught. Teachers will find that the arts can be integrated very naturally within this model; the framework provides a structure that enables all learners to become involved in the learning process.

Before describing the model, it is important to set the stage. During the 1980s, researchers examined the ways students and adults learn. As an outcome of this research, many inventories were devised to enable people to learn more about the way they prefer to learn—their "learning style." Prominent in this area of inquiry is Bernice McCarthy, Director of Excel, Inc., in Barrington, Illinois. In December 1979, Dr. McCarthy convened a group of prominent people from various fields, including medicine, the arts, psychology, business, and education. As a result of this conference, she published the first of a series of books—*The 4Mat System: Teaching to Learning Styles with Right/Left Mode Techniques* (6). A basis for her system was the area of hemisphericity—left and right brain functions.

Hemisphericity began with physiological and psychological research. During the 1950s, Roger Sperry conducted a series of experiments upon animals in which he severed the corpus callosum, the cable of nerves that cross-connects the two cerebral hemispheres (cited in McCarthy [6]). As he observed the animals whose brains were split, he found that although there was no great change in behavior, the animals demonstrated two independent minds—each with its own recognition, memory, and decision system. In the 1960s, similar operations were performed upon patients suffering from severe epilepsy. Patients whose brains were split had their attacks under control, as the attacks were fewer and the patients were able to function without outward disabilities. A series of tests was devised to find out what was happening in the two separated hemispheres. The results were similar to those conducted upon animals.

Joseph Bogen, an associate of Dr. Sperry and a major contributor at the 1979 conference (6), indicated that the implications of Sperry's work were extremely important for education. For example:

- The two halves of the brain process information differently.
- In the split-brain patient, there seemed to be two different people—each with favorite ways of processing information, each with a different mode of thinking.
- Both hemispheres are equally important.

As Dr. McCarthy stated, "What we educators need to do is to develop teaching methodologies which will effectively teach to both modes" (6, p. 73).

Each hemisphere processes information in its own way. The left side of the brain processes it sequentially, analytically, serially, rationally. The right side of the brain, however, grasps whole ideas, sees patterns and connections, understands intuitively. The qualities of each hemisphere are delineated below:

Left Mode (logical)	*Right Mode* (intuitive)
verbal	nonverbal
rational	nonrational
abstract	analogic
symbolic	concrete
analytic	holistic
digital	spatial

The following list of associations and analogies reflects the essence of each hemisphere:

Left Hemisphere	*Right Hemisphere*
Sees the trees	Sees the forest
Detective	Fortune teller
Scheduled	Open-ended/Flexible
Mozart Symphony	Jazz
Haiku/Cinquain	Free verse

Neat desk	Cluttered desk
Calligraphy	Eclectic script
Tennis	Bicycling
Piet Mondrian	Jackson Pollack
Popular Mechanics	*People* Magazine
Planned vacation	Serendipitous expedition
Business suit	Free-flowing clothes
Timekeeper	Watchless
Recipe cooking	Creating a new dish
Scrabble	Boggle
Verbal directions	Map

Each individual has a favorite way of processing information. David Kolb, another major contributor to the 1979 conference, constructed his Learning Style Inventory to help people understand their styles of learning. After conducting extensive tests, he found that people tend to fall in one of four categories: (1) those who perceive concretely and process reflectively—sensors/feelers and watchers; (2) those who perceive abstractly and process reflectively—thinkers and watchers; (3) those who perceive abstractly and process actively—thinkers and doers; (4) those who perceive concretely and process actively—sensors/feelers and doers (4).

A particular learning style is thus a combination of the way one perceives information and the way one processes it. Some people perceive through the senses—others through the intellect. If we think of learning style as a continuum of thinking processes and attributes, each individual stands somewhere on a line between concrete and abstract:

Concrete _____ Abstract

Sensors tend to be closer to the concrete end of the line; thinkers tend to be closer to the abstract end. Sensors are people who need to focus upon tangible materials and concrete experiences, build upon what they already know, discuss things with others. Thinkers are comfortable with concepts and ideas that they glean from the books they read or directly from experts.

Processing is making the information that we have perceived a part of ourselves. The continuum is from active to reflective:

Active _____ Reflective

Doers want to use the information immediately. They want to try it out, experiment with it, touch it, tinker with it, engage their senses in the process of learning. Reflecters need time to think about what they are learning before they go ahead. They watch and listen, making sure that they understand fully. Only then are they ready to try it for themselves, to use the materials or to work with the information.

The classroom teacher should acknowledge all styles of learning. Working upon the basic assumption that the classroom contains all four kinds of learners and that successful instruction must address each type, Dr. McCarthy constructed the 4Mat System, using left/right mode techniques and teaching to all types of learners. She stresses that each style is equally valuable. The difference between the styles is based upon the way individuals perceive and process information. The McCarthy model may be visualized as indicated by Figure 3. The characteristics of the learning style within each quadrant, delineated by the numbers in the figure, Dr. McCarthy posits, are as follows:

1's favorite question is ''Why?''
  learn by feeling and watching.
  are interested in personal meaning.
  need to know WHY they are learning to be motivated.
  respond to the discussion method of teaching.

2's favorite question is ''What?''
  learn by watching and thinking.
  are interested in facts, research, theory.
  respond to the information method of teaching.

3's favorite question is ''How?''
  learn by thinking and doing.
  are interested in process.
  respond to the coaching method of teaching.

4's favorite question is ''If...then?''
  learn by sensing and doing.
  respond to the self-discovery method of teaching.
  need to take what they have learned and make it their own.

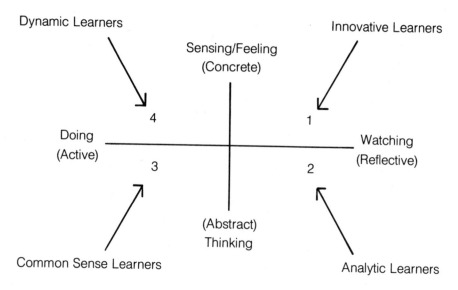

Figure 3
Types of Learners and Learning Styles

These findings relate directly to the way teachers interact with students. The implications address diversity in teaching, as well as in learning. In many of our schools, the 2's are the learners who do well. They feel comfortable most of the time, while the rest of the students (perhaps three-quarters of them) do not. If each student is to feel validated and be successful, teachers must vary their approaches, their repertoire or teaching strategies. They must incorporate a general approach that will enable every learner to shine at least some of the time. New approaches will address students' strengths as well as their weaknesses. As they see and use their strengths, their confidence will grow and they will be open to venture, to risk, and to demonstrate skills and talents that no one might ever have known they possessed. They will also find new strengths upon which they can build to overcome weaknesses, which they will, in turn, strengthen.

The 4Mat System is a teaching model that consciously shifts from the left to the right mode and sequentially progresses from the concrete to the abstract, from the reflective to the active. Throughout the process, both teacher and learner enter each of the four quadrants.

During the course of study, the teacher progresses from motivator to presenter to coach and then to remediator/evaluator. Students progress from discussing/sharing to listening/imaging/ absorbing information to experimenting/tinkering/applying to adapting/enriching the information—teaching it to themselves and then to others.

This process also requires that both thinking modes, left and right, be actively engaged. The teacher begins where students are by setting the stage—creating a concrete experience in which all are engaged. This is followed by an analysis of the experience. The teacher then moves into the next phase, shifting back to the right mode and presenting the concepts using visualization and imagery—showing the big picture. The next step is to present the concepts and skills in a logical, sequential manner (left mode). Now students are ready to try out their newly acquired skills. They continue in the left mode and practice, test things out, applying their newly acquired skills so they will not lose them. The teacher serves as a coach, entering in when needed. The shift to the right mode occurs when students add something of their own to the learning, which is no longer in the same form as it was when the teacher presented it. The learners are now ready to analyze it for its relevance, plan to teach it to their peers or others, and decide how to enhance the ideas/concepts. They might take it into another area—from mathematics into dramatics, from reading into writing, from social studies into art and music. Meanwhile, the teacher continually evaluates students' experiences and remediates, if necessary.

The final aspect of the process takes the learning back into students' lives. How they take the learning and make it their own is their unique challenge. As they work, they elevate their learning to a higher level. They start with the present and end by taking their experiences into the future, as the concepts and skills become incorporated.

Throughout the process, students progress from the concrete to the abstract with respect to the curricular material. They proceed from reflective observation to active experimentation as they think about what they are learning and then actually utilize materials, augmenting them and enriching their products, as well as themselves as learners.

Figure 4 illustrates a unit integrating the arts with the 4Mat System. It features Butterflies as a course of study for use in kindergarten through second grade.

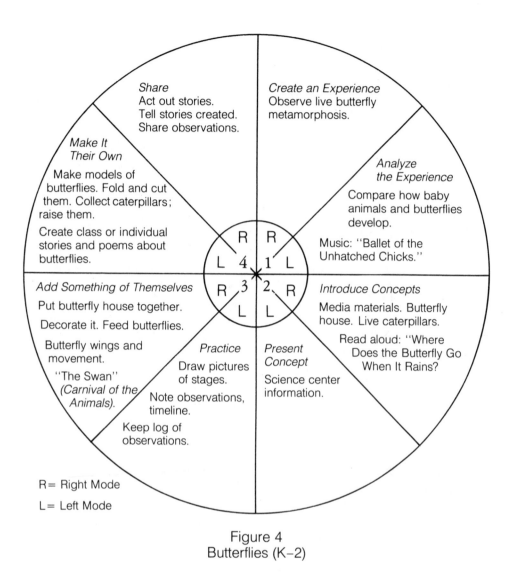

Figure 4
Butterflies (K–2)

ILLUSTRATIVE UNITS

Butterflies

The purpose of the unit was to have the children observe the process of metamorphosis and understand the three stages. The teacher began by having children watch as the butterfly emerged from its cocoon. They made observations and engaged in a discussion of the sequence of the transformation.

Dialogue/discussion is a key component of the initial stage; children are motivated to find out the answers to the why questions. They discuss what they already know, what they think they know, and what they would like to know.

Children were led into the next stage by analyzing the experience. The teacher compiled a list of their observations and then asked them to think about comparing baby animals' development to that of the butterfly. Listening to a piece of music, they responded with a movement activity, flitting gracefully around the room.

The next step was to listen to a story read aloud, "Where Does the Butterfly Go When It Rains?" in preparation for learning about these insects. A large framed "cage"—a butterfly house—was displayed so that the children could observe live caterpillars. The teacher presented scientific information about how the caterpillar is transformed into a butterfly. Children immediately drew pictures of what they had just been taught. They painted, they sketched, they cut and pasted—all art forms relating to the unit. As they became more actively involved, the teacher became less a presenter and more a facilitator.

Then the children decided that they would like to construct their own butterfly house. They decorated it, fed their butterflies, and danced to the strains of Schumann's "Papillons," a delicate piece, like the wings of a butterfly.

The last step found the children making construction paper models of butterflies and decorating the room with their models—hanging them from the ceiling. They collected caterpillars and placed them in the house. They wrote individual and group stories about butterflies; they wrote poetry and published it. They made up stories and acted them out using mime, movement, artwork, and butterfly models.

Art and music played an integral role within the unit. The scientific aspects were deepened and broadened. As children drew, the experience of metamorphosis was memorialized. As their senses were engaged, they visualized metamorphosis. They crawled like caterpillars, climbed into their cocoons, slept, and emerged as beautiful butterflies. When they engaged in dramatic play, they painted a mural as a backdrop. Art was a key component as they worked through each step along the way.

It is important to note that when learners understand the material, they can demonstrate their understanding by presenting it in a variety of ways—using metaphors, writing songs/stories/poetry about the theme/course of study. Incorporating the arts deepens the learner's experience, activates the senses, and enriches the curriculum. The arts make it possible for nonverbal students to exhibit their knowledge using nonverbal modalities. One area of the curriculum builds upon another. Concepts are reinforced. Connections are made, linking the learner to the material. This is demonstrated in the learning process, as well as in students' products.

So much of schoolwork depends upon the ability to communicate with words. For some students this is easily accomplished; for others it ranges from difficult to nearly impossible. The arts allow all students to participate and to show others what they know.

It is vital that children experience the shift from one mode to another within a period of time that refreshes the learner. When they are engaged in an activity of one mode for more than an hour and a half, fatigue sets in and productivity lessens. When they take tests, for example, they need a break to refresh and restore their ability to concentrate. After singing, they can turn to a writing or reading activity with full energy. If they are working with technical details, after a period of time they need to shift to an activity that is more global—an arts experience, listening to a story or a piece of music, moving their bodies to a rhythmic beat. Then they shift again to a sequential activity such as writing. They come to this new activity with energy, restored and refreshed after working in the right mode. As they begin to write, they are in the left mode. The effect is the same as doing calisthenics and then sitting down to work at a desk; it is calisthenics of the mind.

Sun Time

This unit is a study of the sun as it relates to time, designed for use in grades three through five. It begins with an experience—students observing their shadows—and then moves around the circle clockwise, as students are introduced to sundials, gather materials to make them, construct a sun dial, paint a mural involving shadows and sundials, calibrate and use a sundial, and then teach others about sundials.

Figure 5 demonstrates the shift in modes as students turn from observing their shadows to analyzing them—testing shadows at different times of the day, noting their length and position. They shift into concept development by first watching slides and then reading about shadows, sun, sundials. They shift again by listening to a presentation/lecture about how sundials are constructed and how they are used. The next shift is to an active mode—making their own sundials. They paint their dials, exercising both creativity and technical skills. In another shift, they add writing, art, and music to their course of study. The final shifts are calibrating their sundials, writing a user's guide, and then taking their sundials home to use with their families.

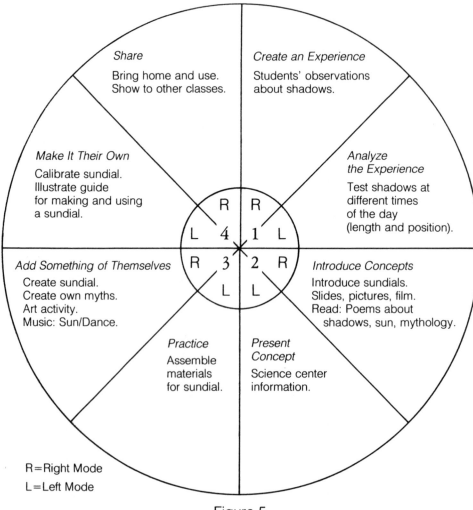

Figure 5
Sun Shadows/Sun Time (Grades 3–5)

Chapter 4

CLASSROOM APPLICATIONS

Every September a new planbook—a book with squares to be filled in—finds its way to the teacher's desk. Language arts, social studies, reading, mathematics, art, music, physical education, and health are placed within the squares. This method of planning, however, fragments, compartmentalizes, isolates each area. Rather than separating subjects, we should create bridges from one subject or activity to another. Reading, for example, takes place not only during "reading period," but also during other times, including social studies and mathematics. The "reading" activity can incorporate spelling, vocabulary, social studies concepts, music, art, movement, mathematics. Each subject area has within it elements from all the others. To integrate the curriculum, the teacher has to recognize the possibilities for connection making and capitalize upon them (e.g., American history and quilting, mythology and science, music and literature, drama and grammar). The mosaic of the curriculum enlarges, title by title, piece by piece, interlocking to emerge as a unified whole. Poems of shadows are incorporated into a mathematics lesson; Stonehenge and moon calendars become both art and science lessons. A physical education exercise can be incorporated into a science project on the human skeleton. Through these approaches, teachers and students begin to think holistically. They see patterns, they understand the big picture. The following units illustrate both the integration of the arts and the 4Mat System.

THREE UNITS

The Battle of the Blue and Gray: U.S. Civil War (Grade 5)
(contributed by Jill Endicott and Tonni Giguiere, Teachers, Green Valley Elementary School, Danville, California)

Introduction

The unit began with a visit to the class by a man dressed as Abraham Lincoln, who talked to students as if they were living in the 1860s. The students learned many facts about living conditions during that time and asked "Abe" numerous questions. After the visitor left, they analyzed the experience—listing what they already knew, what they would like to know, and what they thought they knew about the U.S. Civil War.

Students created a web of interrelated areas to explore. It included people such as Abraham Lincoln, Ulysses S. Grant, Robert E. Lee, Harriet Tubman, Jefferson Davis, Stonewall Jackson, Stephen A. Douglass, Sojourner Truth, John Brown, General G. B. McClellan, Harriet Beecher Stowe, Major General William T. Sherman, James E. B. Stuart, Matthew Brady, Major General George H. Thomas, John Wilkes Booth. They also wanted to find out about the South, cotton, plantations, slavery, the Confederacy, customs, costumes, foods, dances, music of the time, the army, the North, the Union. All these topics were listed as they were articulated.

Activities

Of special note in this unit was the personal involvement of all students in the assignments that involved the integration of subject matter into a unified whole. They were asked to choose one of the people, do research, write a major report about the person and his/her times, and then give a speech to the class as if they were that person, outlining his/her career highlights. If they wished, they could create a period costume to wear when they made their presentation. Within the body of the research report they were to use illustrations, drawings, sketches, maps, and charts. Their readings included *The Red Badge of Courage,* by Stephen Crane; *Uncle Tom's Cabin,* by Harriet Beecher Stowe; *Across Five Aprils,* by Irene Hunt.

Students listened as the teacher read aloud "The Gettysburg Address," "Barbara Fritchie," "Sheridan's Ride," and "O Captain, My Captain" during the course of the unit. They chose one of these works and memorized it. They wrote poems of their own. Their drawings reflected the knowledge gleaned from their readings. It provided an opportunity for them to take what they had learned and depict it in another mode. When a student incorporates a concept, it is possible to demonstrate it in another way. Rather than parrot back what the teacher has said or what was just read, the learner takes the information and personalizes it—takes ownership of it and presents it in a new way. Life as art; art as life. Some students, for example, made clay models of a plantation, of soldiers on the battlefield, or of people dressed in the fashions of the time.

Optional activities were also chosen for enrichment/extra credit: a Civil War newspaper, including editorials, cartoons, advertisements; a list of Civil War songs, including original songs containing important facts about the war.

Before students presented their products, the teachers became coaches and helped them find the resources they needed to be successful. They used their social studies textbook as background material and were given a test after completing their assigned readings and research.

The culmination of the unit was their special project, which students presented in class for their peers to learn from and enjoy. They were able to "walk in another pair of shoes"; they became the person they had chosen to depict. By engaging in the dynamic experience of becoming someone else, that person's beliefs came alive to students. They related history to the present as they analyzed the impact of the Civil War upon the economic development of the United States, the effect of freeing the slaves upon the people of the South and the rest of the country. They looked at what has happened to the South since those times and conjectured what it might have been like if the outcome had been different. Critical thinking skills, analytical discussions, dramatic moments, musical memories—each aspect made a bridge to the next. The whole was greater than the sum of the parts: synergy/energy.

All students, regardless of learning style, were able to be successful. The doers had opportunities to engage in activities and also to be reflective and analytical. The thinkers rejoiced in their research and also stretched their skills by engaging in hands-on activities. The dreamers were able to make up their own songs, write their own skits, publish their newspaper. And the concrete learners who thrive on discussion were able to work cooperatively on their projects and learn from each other. Throughout this whole project, everyone was taken through each stage by the skillful orchestration of the teachers, who were, in turn, motivators, presenters, coaches, and evaluators/remediators.

The teachers felt the unit was successful beyond the classroom: "The results of this unit were very positive. The students' interest peaked. It reached out into the dinner conversation. Their poetry was beautiful, artwork was appealing, writings were filled with feeling and compassion. Their research skills were sharpened, memory heightened, reading interest was high, oral language and listening skills were developed, and their creativity was challenged."

Pirates in the Kindergarten

(contributed by Jill Endicott, Teacher, Green Valley Elementary School, Danville, California)

This integrated unit contains the elements of drama, music, literature, poetry, mathematics, art, crafts, media, dramatic play, movement, and nutrition.

The kindergartners were studying the "letter of the week." When they came to "X," the teacher wrote a big X on a small piece of paper and placed it atop the book *Pigwig and the Pirates*, by John Dyke. As they listened to the story, students were introduced to pirate language (e.g., "Shiver me timbers ... slit me gizzard!... Yo ho ho ..."). They talked about the story and then looked at pictures of pirates from the pages of Robert Louis Stevenson's *Treasure Island*.

After the story time, they learned some pirate songs—"Fifteen Men on a Dead Man's Chest" and "Three Pirates Came to London Town." They shifted into a more active mode by swaggering around the room like pirates and walking the plank.

During free play, the children created an island on a sand table and pretended they were pirates who lived there. They practiced writing X's in the sand, singing their pirate songs as they worked.

The next story they heard during the week of this unit was "Peter Pan." They learned to sing "Tender Shepherd," "I've Gotta Crow," "I Won't Grow Up," and "Captain Hook's Waltz" from the musical *Peter Pan*. They moved liked Peter and pretended to fly.

As part of the whole-language approach, they wrote stories—"My Pirate Adventure"—and illustrated them. Some children were able to write their thoughts using invented spelling; others dictated the words for the teacher to write underneath their pictures.

They made pirate hats—three-cornered, decorated with a skull and crossbones—and wore them as they engaged in free play during the morning. When they went to the school library, they borrowed some of the pirate picture books the librarian had collected for them to read in their classroom.

As part of the social studies curriculum, the children had made a map of their school. They showed landmarks by pasting on the map pictures they had drawn of the cafeteria, the auditorium, the bathrooms, the principal's office, the health room, other classrooms, and the playground. Later, when they found that an X had been placed on the map, they were told that at the end of the week they would have a surprise—they would go on a treasure hunt.

On Friday, they donned their pirate hats and began their trek to find the buried treasure. They started where the X was—outside their classroom. On the reverse side of that paper and others was a little note telling them where to go next. They counted the notes as they went along. They counted the number of steps they took to go from one place to another. Then they came to the last X, which said, "X marks the spot!" And there was the treasure—"Pirates on a Plank"—stalks of celery filled with peanut butter and dotted with raisins.

The children brought their treasures back to the classroom and had a party, singing songs and listening to their favorite stories reread by the teacher. When work period came, some children chose to paint pirate pictures in tempera at the easel. Others worked on simple pirate puzzles, while a group of young designers built a pirate ship out of their big blocks and invited everyone to come aboard.

Helping children to understand their world and find clues in nature, as well as within the school, the teacher took the class on a field trip the following week. They were to look for signs of animals and to count how many different animals they saw along the way. They found all kinds of nests and holes in the ground; they heard birds sing, dogs bark, crickets chirp, squirrels scold. Returning to the classroom, they talked about what they had seen and heard, what they had sensed and smelled. Their critical thinking skills were challenged as they raised questions that took them beyond the initial experience. This activity flowed from the initial pirate unit—from the fanciful to the real, from make-believe to believe. The arts were always the central core of the curriculum.

The children wanted to record what they had seen, so they went to their easels and crayons, their fingerpaints and clay. Their products reflected their insights and interpretations of their environment. Just like the pirates looking for buried treasure, they became scientists finding evidence and making sense of it.

The sequence of this unit was to start with a concrete experience, learn the facts, take the facts and play with them, incorporate them into the children's repertoire, create new materials (original stories and plays), and then celebrate with a field event that began the cycle of learning all over again.

Throughout the unit, teacher and children addressed the following questions:

- Why am I learning/teaching this?
- What are the facts and concepts I want to learn/teach?
- How can I test out what I have learned/taught?
- If I do this . . . THEN what will happen?

The 4Mat cycle of learning and teaching is designed to help students proceed from the concrete to the abstract, from the reflective to the active mode, ending with a product of the learner's making.

Casey at the Bat (Grade 6)

(contributed by Jeryl Abelmann, Teacher, Green Valley Elementary School, Danville, California)

Since every spring people thrill to the opening of the baseball season, the purpose of this unit was to integrate happenings outside the classroom with happenings within. Baseball was the unifying element. Within the course of a few weeks, students explored the history of the game, linking it to music, art, poetry, and public speaking. The objectives were to expose students to poetry and have them learn to make their own interpretations by reading aloud. They learned how to use the library's reference services and do research to learn the history of baseball. They planned a slide/tape program and produced it, presenting it to the school on the opening day of the baseball season. They selected music to accompany the slides and learned the songs. They used their graphic skills to punctuate the poetry reading.

The unit began with a reading of three poems—"Casey at the Bat," "Casey's Revenge," and "Casey 20 Years Later." At the outset, the teacher dramatized the three poems. Students read them again, part by part, selecting the parts they wanted to draw. They illustrated their selections to accompany the poetry; their drawings were made into slides. The slides were numbered and placed in order with the tape so that each slide synchronized with the reading.

Each student practiced reading a section of the poems and the class rehearsed acting them out. The poetry readings were taped. Students sang "Take Me Out to the Ballgame," which was also taped and added as a background to the slide/tape using a mixer. At the same time, students compiled data from their research and learned about the history of baseball. Each student submitted a one- to two-page report with illustrations.

In addition, students wrote their own poems using the same rhythm as "Casey" and the name of their hometown. They were directed to their newspaper's sports section for references to Casey and Mudville. They read the biography of Daniel Henry Casey, the "real" Casey. They learned how fiction and fact came together and began to understand how writers find their inspiration.

During physical education classes students formed two teams and held practices between Mudville and Bugville. On the big day, the opening of the baseball season, parents were invited to attend the assembly to watch the slide/tape, hear students sing, listen to their reports about the history of baseball, and watch the final game between Mudville and Bugville. The unit was enriched by baseball food—hotdogs cooked in a solar cooker.

The performing and graphic arts were a central core of this unit, uniting the mind and the body, sports and history, drama and poetry, music and movement, reading and writing. One area connected to another, forming an integrated whole.

Chapter 5

FOR SPACIOUS SKIES
(An Extended Study)

The true journey of discovery
consists not in finding new landscapes, but in having new eyes.
—Marcel Proust

We have always a resource in
the skies. They are constantly
turning a new page to view. The
wind sets the type in this blue
ground and the inquiring may always read the new truth.
—Henry David Thoreau

The sky—a unifying element, accessible to all, a source of inspiration, a catalyst, a stimulus, an appropriate focus at any level—
has been a subject that the authors have explored in depth during
the past six years. Working with students at every level, from nurs-
ery school through graduate school, we have seen what can happen
when teachers bring the sky into the classroom.

GETTING STARTED

Thoughts for the teacher: Start with yourself. What does the sky
mean to you? Feelings, thoughts, wonderings, dreams. What do
you know about the sky? Answer for yourself, ''Why am I interested in the sky? Why do I want to introduce this to my students?''
Start by looking up. Give yourself time to observe, to concentrate,

46

to focus, to listen, smell, feel, see, and to record your thoughts and feelings in a journal. See what happens when you do this on a regular basis.

The next questions to ask yourself are, "What do I want to teach my students? Which concepts, skills, songs, stories, art experiences, films, tapes do I want to incorporate and utilize? How can I weave mathematics, music, meteorology, mythology together to form a pattern within the fabric of my course of study?" Gather your resources and integrate the subjects: science, social studies, economics, poetry, drawing, painting, sculpture, weaving, literature, astronomy, art, prose, agriculture, horticulture, architecture, physical education, letterwriting. As you work one subject into another, students' understanding deepens and their lives become enriched. The learning is connected to the self. The quest for knowledge becomes a joyous, fascinating adventure.

The third phase is the doing. "How do I do this?" the student asks. "Let me try it out, test, experiment, tinker." Providing for hands-on experiences is the essence of this phase. Students must have firsthand opportunities; they must use their kinesthetic sense to try out their newly acquired knowledge and understandings in various ways. They write, they draw, they construct, they work with concrete materials.

Then, if they have learned the material, they can take their knowledge and make it their own, adapting, enriching, augmenting, linking it to their lives and to the future. They can make it something greater, deeper, broader than it was and teach it to someone else.

Choose a day with a bright blue sky, preferably one with large, puffy clouds. Pull down the shades in your room or ask students to close their eyes and describe how the sky looked on the way to school. If the students can write, pass out paper and ask them to write their observations. Based upon the authors' experience, there will be more silence than words and more blank paper than full paragraphs. After a few minutes, ask students to put their papers aside and go outdoors. Tell them to find a place on the playground and just look at the sky for a few minutes—no talking, just looking. Then have them return to the classroom and write (or talk about) what they have just seen. You should do it, too. Students and teacher then share what they have seen. This leads quite naturally into journal writing, as in the following examples:

Sky Observation—Journal Entry #14—Drew Prairie,
Grade Five, Vista Grande School, Danville, California

The sky is like a motionless sea. The few clouds streamy-like, remind me of the great surfers, riding the great white wave. There is a slight breeze, not a breeze where you need a jacket, but one that sends a chill down your spine. The sun is out; it's shining on us all with its golden rays, making us feel good. The trees are swaying, as if expecting a storm or bad weather. Today is a wonderful day for fun and play.

Sky Observation—Journal Entry #14—Michelle Malsbary,
Grade Five, Vista Grande School, Danville, California

Today the sky was blue. It was a very light clear blue. There were very thin stratus clouds that almost blended in with the cheerful blue sky. There were also some thicker stratus clouds. It seemed as if pure white icing was spread across a blue cake. The sight I saw was so spectacular it was hard to explain clearly. When the sky is like this, I feel free.

It is important to find out what students already know as you embark upon a new course of study. Webbing or mapping is an approach that encourages brainstorming, reflective thought, and creative thinking.

Write the word SKY on a large sheet of newsprint and ask students what they think of when they think about the sky. As they brainstorm their one-word responses, link them where they fit, categorizing as you go along. Figure 6 illustrates a section of a fifth grade class's web.

After the web has been constructed, post it on the wall and keep adding to it as you go along. As you discuss what students already know, make a list of what they think they know and what they want to know. Investment of students in their own learning is the key to their involvement, to enabling them to think, to plan, and to organize their thoughts.

Sky journal entries should become part of students' daily work. As students begin to see how the sky is ever-changing—how it has so many colors, how the clouds move across it, how it has many objects, how students can become more aware of different sights

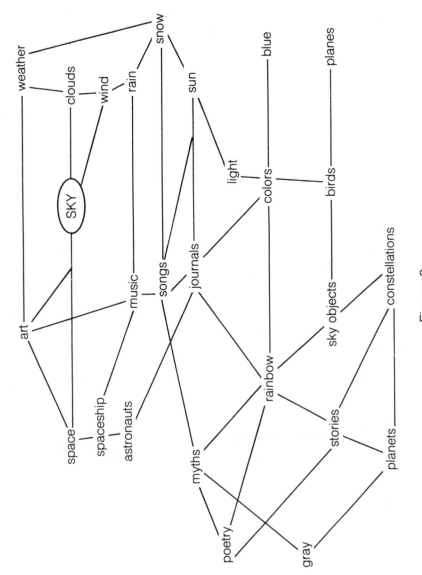

Figure 6
Fifth Grade Class Web

49

and smells, thoughts and feelings—you will notice their language becoming enriched, their descriptive ability improving, their fluency and sentence structure becoming more complex.

INTEGRATED ACTIVITIES FOR MUSIC

Teach sky songs matching the subject as you go along. For example, when studying weather, teach songs relating to the weather. A list of appropriate pieces follows.

- *Sunrise:* Sibelius's "Night Ride and Sunrise," Opus 55; "Sunrise, Sunset" from *Fiddler on the Roof;* Hovaness's "Sunrise."
- *Sunset:* Respighi's "The Sunset," "Red Sails in the Sunset," "Deep Purple Night," Mussorgsky's "Night on Bald Mountain," "Moscow Nights," Berlioz's "The Nights of Summer."
- *Stars:* "When You Wish Upon a Star," "The Star-Spangled Banner," "Twinkle, Twinkle, Little Star."
- *Moon:* "Moonglow," Crumb's "The Night of the Four Moons," "Aiken Drum."
- *Sky:* "Blue Skies," "Skylark," "Dites-Moi" from *South Pacific.*
- *Wind:* "The Breeze and I," "You'll Never Walk Alone," "They Call the Wind Maria."
- *Rain:* "April Showers," "Soon It's Gonna Rain" from *The Fantasticks,* "Raindrops Keep Fallin' on My Head."

As students are working on projects or reading quietly, play soft classical music in the background.

Have students move to the music. For example, they could be clouds drifting along as they listen to George Winston's "Autumn" album. This connects to their study of cloud types, or to their journal writing on a particularly cloudy day.

Invite musicians in to the class to play pieces associated with the sky. They might be students' parents or the students themselves.

As students listen to the music, they could be sketching or drawing designs or subjects that are stimulated by the sounds they are hearing. During art classes, music could be playing. It sets a mood, a tone, a feeling that deepens the experience.

INTEGRATED ACTIVITIES FOR VISUAL ARTS

Visit your local art museum with your class. Have students view paintings of the great masters that have spectacular skies, stormy skyscapes, ethereal skies, cityscapes, landscapes, seascapes, night skies, early morning skies. Have them choose some of their favorite paintings; purchase slides of some of these paintings at the museum shop and bring them back to the classroom. Add a tape of James Galway's flute pieces, and you have a slide/tape program that is a powerful collection to use in a variety of ways.

- Students can compare the different styles of the painters and learn about their lives as they find their biographies in the library.
- Students can view each painting and write about their feelings and thoughts as they view the slides slowly and reflectively.
- The art specialist can teach students how to depict skies using various media—watercolors, pastels, tempera, fingerpaints. They can learn printmaking and make sky murals.

Local museums often contain resources for schools. The Museum of Fine Arts in Boston, for example, has slides for sale. Among the artists represented are van Ruisdael, Monet, Boudin, Gérôme to Bierstadt, Bellows, Whistler, Turner, and Church. Slides include Allston's *Moonlight Landscape and Rising of a Thunderstorm at Sea,* George Bellows' *Sea,* Monet's *Poplars,* Bierstadt's *Thunderstorm in the Rocky Mountains,* Boudin's *Venice—The Salute from San Giorgio,* and Turner's *Slave Ship.*

In addition to use in the art activities suggested above, the slides can serve as a stimulus for creative writing, for inspiration, for reflective thinking. They can be used to provide inspiration for writing poetry, for writing big books. The stormy pictures may help students who are studying the Pilgrims write a simulated journal as if they themselves were making the perilous crossing on the *Mayflower.* The slides could also serve as a background for a concert devoted to sky songs. And they could be used to teach students about the environment—comparing the sky in the paintings to the sky over the city after the morning rush hour.

Looking at the sky within the framework of the 4Mat approach, the sequence of activities begins with the daily sky observations, journal writing, vocabulary building. It extends into students' activities—finding sky references in their readings, bringing in magazine and newspaper references to the sky, finding examples of how the sky is used in advertising, making collages of clipped sky pictures and classifying them according to type—evening, sunset, clear skies, stormy weather. Such activities help students think critically, analyze, and classify.

As the class proceeds into all aspects of the curriculum, you can use the sky as a unifier. In math, students can graph the time the sun rises and sets daily and figure out the number of hours of sunlight. They can estimate the time the sun will set and then check the newspaper to see how close they came. They can consult the weather channel and record the weather on a daily basis, charting the temperature, wind velocity, humidity. They can make predictions and construct weather instruments.

Students are filled with wonder; they are naturally curious. They question and ponder. Building upon this, they can list the questions suggested by thinking about the sky: Why is the sky blue? How did the Big Dipper get there? What causes thunder? How did the sky get its colors? Their questions can form the basis of a study of mythology. You can read sky-related myths to the class. Then students can write their own myths to answer their wonderings. For example, the person who asked about the Big Dipper can write a story about it. Integrating the creative writing with artwork, students can illustrate their books and then bind them carefully so that they will last. They can read their books to their peers and to others in the school.

As the curriculum unfolds, one area merges with another. It is organic, a coming together, not a fragmentation. The teacher brings things together, connecting the elements and linking the learning. It is a collective effort of classroom teacher, students, subject area specialists, volunteers, parents, administrators. These collaborations will reap a rich harvest.

The sky provides a rich field for scientific inquiry. Students learn about the solar system, the spectrum, ecology, environmental issues, aerodynamics, how to use a telescope, astronomy, and time. They can learn how to construct a sundial—an activity that integrates mathematics and science, as well as graphics.

STUDENT AND STAFF PRODUCTS

Our Big Sky Book

(contributed by Lynn Hunt,
Kindergarten Teacher,
Natick, Massachusetts)

Astronaut, astronaut
What do you see?
I see a spaceship looking at me.

Spaceship, spaceship
What do you see?
I see a star looking at me.

Star, star
What do you see?
I see the moon looking at me.

Moon, moon
What do you see?
I see a planet looking at me.

Planet, planet
What do you see?
I see Halley's Comet looking at me.

Halley's Comet, Halley's Comet
What do you see?
I see aliens looking at me.

Aliens, aliens
What do you see?
We see the sun looking at us.

Sun, sun
What do you see?
I see EVERYONE looking at me—

    an astronaut,
    a spaceship,
    a star,
    a moon,
    a planet,
    Halley's Comet and
    aliens!

Look Up!

(contributed by Steve Gould, Principal,
Briggs School, Ashburnham, Massachusetts)

Look up! The sky's amazin'.
Look up! It's always changin'.
It's gonna be a great day.
Look up! The sun is shining.
Look up! There's no denying
It's gonna be a great day.

Oh, look at the sky! Oh my!
Oh, look at the *_____! Oh my!
Oh, look at the *_____! Oh my!
The sky, oh my!

Look up! The sky's amazin'.
Look up! It's always changin'.
It's gonna be a great night.
Look up! The moon is growing.
Look up! The stars are showing.
It's gonna be a great night.

Oh, look at the sky! Oh my!
Oh, look at the *_____! Oh my!
Oh, look at the *_____! Oh my!
The sky, oh my!

Look up! The sky's amazin'.
Look up! It's always changin'.
It's gonna be a wet day.
Look up! The rain is coming.
Look up! The clouds are grumbling.
It's gonna be a wet day.

Oh, look at the sky! Oh my!
Oh, look at the *_____! Oh my!
Oh, look at the *_____! Oh my!
The sky, oh my!

Look up! The sky's amazin'.
Look up! It's always changin'.
It's gonna be a great day.
Look up! The sun is shining.
Look up! There's no denying
It's gonna be a great day.

*Students provide the words that they associate with ☐ Sunny sky: birds, kites; ☐ Evening sky: Milky Way, Big Dipper; ☐ Rainy/snowy sky: storm, rainbow.

Clouds

(contributed by Drew Prairie, Grade Five,
Vista Grande School, Danville, California)

Have you looked up today
And seen what I have seen?
You do not just see blue and white,
For if you look hard enough
You might have seen what I have seen.

You never look right into the sky
Because you will miss its beauty.
You must lie down and gaze with all your might.
The sky is filled with many wonderful things—
Things only you can see.

For I have seen castles.
My friend has seen men.
But all who don't believe in me—
The non-dreamers and believers . . .
They shall never see what I have seen—
For they are the non-believers.

CONCLUSION

And now we come to the end of this chapter—a chapter that continues to be written in the planbooks of teachers throughout the country, teachers who have seen what happens both to students and to themselves when they integrate their teaching and learning.

Drew Prairie made the connection in his philosophical poem:

Life Is Like a Room

Life is like a room.
You learn math, a door opens in your room.
Now you can enter another room.
Yet, I dislike rooms.
I like to be free outside, and now I am.
For the door to the sky was opened for me.
Now I can leave the rooms and go outside.
This door is the only door out of the room.
Because of it, For Spacious Skies,
Life is not just a room.
It is a whole world of sky magic.

55

BIBLIOGRAPHY

1. Efland, Arthur. "Excellence in Education: The Role of the Arts." In *Fine Arts in the Curriculum,* edited by Frederick B. Tuttle, Jr., pp. 11–15. Washington, D.C.: National Education Association, 1985.
2. Eisner, Elliot. "Why Arts Are Basic." *Basic Education* 31, no. 9 (May 1987): 10.
3. Goodlad, John, and Morrison, Jack. "The Arts in Education." In *Art in the Schools*, Institute for the Development of Educational Activities, p. 18. New York: McGraw-Hill, 1980.
4. Kolb, David A.; Rubin, Irwin M.; and McIntyre, James. *Organizational Psychology: A Book of Readings.* 2d ed. Englewood Cliffs, N.J.: Prentice-Hall, 1974.
5. Massachusetts Association for Supervision and Curriculum Development. *Thinking Across the Curriculum.* Acton, Mass.: the Association, 1986.
6. McCarthy, Bernice. *The 4Mat System: Teaching to Learning Styles with Right/Left Mode Techniques.* Barrington, Ill.: Excel, 1980.
7. National Endowment for the Arts. *Toward Civilization: A Report on Arts Education.* Washington, D.C.: U.S. Government Printing Office, 1988.
8. Parker, Elinor, ed. *100 More Story Poems.* New York: Crowell, 1960.
9. Reader's Digest Editors. *Reader's Digest Children's Songbook.* Pleasantville, N.Y.: Reader's Digest Association, 1985.
10. Tuttle, Frederick B., Jr. *Composition: A Media Approach.* Washington, D.C.: National Education Association, 1978.
11. Tuttle, Frederick B., Jr., ed. *Fine Arts in the Curriculum.* Washington, D.C.: National Education Association, 1985.